Joshua-Judges-Ruth

Through the Bible with

Lance Lambert

Joshua
Judges
Ruth

Through the Bible with

Lance Lambert

LANCE LAMBERT MINISTRIES

Richmond, Virginia, USA

ISBN: 978-1-68389-123-9
www.lancelambert.org

Contents

Introduction

This book is part of a series Lance shared at Halford House in Richmond, Surrey, England in which he went through much of the Bible. This series began with an introductory series on how to study the Bible. Many of the studies in both of these series had study guides to accompany them. Our desire is to make these more readily available for reference and study. How to Study the Bible Part 1 and 2 as well as the sections on Genesis to Deuteronomy and Ezra to Esther are currently available in print. You may find these as useful resources to accompany this book. Lord willing, the rest of his series will be forthcoming!

May you be encouraged in the Lord through his ministry and kept until the day of His return as you meet Him in His Word!

With gratitude,
Lance Lambert Ministries team

1.
Joshua

The Historical Section of the Bible

We have previously studied the first five books of the Bible, that five-fold volume that we call the Pentateuch. The whole of the Old Testament and indeed the whole of the rest of the Bible is built upon that five-fold foundation of the Pentateuch. Following those five, the book of Joshua begins a new section: the former and latter prophets. In the Hebrew canon, the "former prophets" are Joshua, Judges, Samuel and Kings. Then there are what they called the "four latter prophets," which are Isaiah, Jeremiah, Ezekiel, and the twelve[1] that were counted as one book. According to our canon, the scriptures that we have, and the arrangement that we have here in our Bible today, it is the beginning of what we call the historical section of the Bible.

---

1 From Hosea to Malachi, the twelve minor prophets

The historical section of the Bible is quite consecutive from Joshua to the book of Esther. That is, it runs right through quite a number of books: Joshua, Judges, Ruth, I and II Samuel, I and II Kings, I and II Chronicles, and then Ezra, Nehemiah, and Esther. That is the historical section of the Old Testament, starting with Joshua.

Now, there are just one or two things that we ought to say. First of all, this historical section of the Old Testament comprises, roughly, about a thousand years of history. It spans a thousand years of God's dealings with His people, and in that thousand years there are three clear phases. Not everyone agrees as to when those phases end and where the new one begins, but all agree that there are three distinct phases in these thousand years of history. The first phase is from Moses to Samuel, the second is from Samuel to the division of Israel, and the third is from the division of Israel to the end of the Old Testament (that is, the prophet Malachi). We have these three distinct phases, and each phase has its own message and illustrates particular principles.

From Moses to Samuel, we have the period of the nation of Israel being constituted and developed. All of God's dealings with them now are to settle them in the land and to instruct them very clearly and deeply as to the nature of their calling as a nation. Therefore, you find that Joshua, Judges, and the beginning of Samuel deal very much with Israel as a nation being settled. You must remember that the Scriptures do not just illustrate by the good points – we have everything also illustrated by failures. In other words, the Scripture uses the contradiction of failures to testify as to what should be, as much as it uses what is good. Consequently, Joshua is overall a good story, and then you get

Judges which on the whole is a positively bad story. Nevertheless, the two do teach us something very wonderful. They teach us those principles upon which God is pleased to lead, vindicate, protect and increase His people.

Then come the books of Samuel and as we go through these books we will begin to see how gradually, book after book builds up until we come to a very difficult overlap of two phases. Here we have the difficulty of deciding where one phase ends and where a new phase begins. For instance, some say, "Oh, Saul is the beginning of the new phase." Others say, "No, David is the beginning of the new phase." One or two say, "Samuel is the beginning of the new phase."

Well, if you look at the Scripture, I think you will probably agree with me that Samuel is the beginning of a new phase. Note that the story of Ruth is inserted in history just to provide us with someone [David] to fill the throne.

Everything moves toward Samuel—Hannah cried for a son. Then Samuel is there as the great turning point in the history of the people, from it just being a nation that was under the rule of God, to it becoming a monarchy. So, the next phase is in Samuel.

I might just add that originally, I and II Samuel and I and II Kings were looked upon as the four books of the kingdom. Therefore, Samuel was included in kingship although he was actually only a judge, a priest, and a prophet. However, we find that with Samuel begins an altogether new phase, and we find that for the first time, Israel has become a monarchy with a king. First, they had a bad king, and then there was a good king. Nevertheless, there begins a royal line. That whole phase up to Solomon is just a moving forward to a great climax. David spent his whole life seeking to build God a house, and you know the climax is reached when Solomon actually builds the house. Then because of Solomon's sin, a terrible thing happened and the nation was rent in two. It would never again, really be properly and genuinely united.

That brings in the third and last great phase of history in the Old Testament: the division of Israel into Israel and Judah—two tribes and ten tribes, both with their kings, and in the end, both with their centres of worship, both rivalling each other and split irrevocably in two. The whole story begins with the decline and the perversion of God's people. In the end, Samaria was carried off into captivity never again to be heard of, and it was followed hundreds of years later by Judah being carried into Babylon. Then the story ends, as you well know, with the remnant coming back in Ezra and Nehemiah's day to rebuild the house and rebuild the walls. Then the prophet Malachi ends these thousand years of history with his great prophecy concerning the sudden coming of the Lord to His temple.

Illustrating the Foundational Principles

We have now left the foundational part of the Bible, the Pentateuch, and have entered the first book of this thousand years of history. That is very, very important for us to understand because this historical section is the building, and the Pentateuch is the foundation. We find here in this historical section the principles contained in the Pentateuch exemplified or illustrated in every way. Continually, you will find that all the way through these thousand years of history, kings and priests and prophets are having to come back to what the Lord said to Moses. They are continually having to say to the people, "You see? Moses said so and so and because we have not done it, this has happened."

So we always find, right the way through, little stories such as when David took up the ark. He forgot! He had never read the book of the Law and he forgot that only Levites were supposed to take the ark on their shoulders and instead it was carried on a cart. The result was having a terrible plague go through the people. So, they left the ark there because so many thousands died in the epidemic. They sought the Lord and when they searched the Scripture, they found it should have been on the shoulders of the Levites. As soon as they put it on the shoulders of the Levites everything was alright.

We find this illustration again and again in this whole thousand years of history. We will find continually that they are having to go back and find out what the Lord said to Moses. In one way or another, we find that they are being continually judged by the Pentateuch. Take Solomon for example. Perhaps you will not realise that all those hundreds of years later when Solomon built his house, he continually harks back to Deuteronomy and what the Lord said about the place that He should choose in which to cause His Name to dwell. There are quite a few chapters that are taken up with just that. Well, we need to see that this whole historical section of the Bible is but the illustration of the principles contained in the Pentateuch.

Then another thing we ought to note is simply that we must not take the title *historical books* or *historical section* too dogmatically because there is actually quite a bit of history in the prophets: Isaiah, Jeremiah, and the others. There is also a large amount of history in the Pentateuch. It is really, I think, a title of convenience more than anything else.

Another thing we ought to make very clear is that it is not history as you and I know history. This history of this thousand years is absolutely remarkable in the things that it includes and the things that it excludes. There are known things of which we would have made a great amount that are just hardly mentioned, if not altogether omitted. Then there are other things like the story of Ruth that we probably would have never thought of including in history, but which the Lord has inserted into history as a very important interlude in it.

So, we have to recognise once again what we have said many times, that the *aim* governs the *scope*. If we are going to try to treat this historical section as history, as we would find in an English textbook, we would be sadly disappointed. This is simply a history from God's standpoint. It therefore brings in and includes everything that in any way affects or realises the divine end.

So, we must view these books from that standpoint. Why does the Lord include that particular history? Why does He make so much of that person or that point of history? It is because here we have the exemplification and the illustration of a principle, and from it, we can learn a tremendous amount.

The Authorship and Date of the Book of Joshua

For the book of Joshua itself, what about its authorship and its date? I think in reading through it, you can see how much of it has been written by an eyewitness. He uses the words "we" and "us," and the way he speaks is very much "we thought."

Another thing you will note is the little phrase "unto this day" that occurs 14 times in the record. "Rahab who lives amongst us unto this day," so it was evidently written in Rahab's lifetime. There are many other things that were said: "unto this day," such as: "remains amongst us unto this day." This clearly reveals to us that a very large part of this book was written by an eyewitness of the things and the events that it records.

Now, do we have any clue as to who is the author of the book of Joshua? Nowhere does Joshua claim to be the author. It says in one or two places that he wrote certain things, and it says certainly that he spoke a lot. Also, we can see quite clearly that he is the main character in the whole story. Jewish tradition asserts very strongly that the author is Joshua, that most of it was material which he wrote, and it was then added to and edited by later scribes. This may well be the truth.

In the very last verses of this book, it speaks of the death of Joshua and says that Israel cleaved to the Lord all the days of Joshua and the days of the elders that outlived Joshua. There is a modern theory that it may be one of those elders who either wrote this book or edited it and added to it. We do not know clearly who it was, but whoever it was must have written it a very short time after the events described and possibly during the actual events themselves.

The book covers a short period of time. It covered only 25 years. As to its date, there is a tremendous amount of controversy. There are two systems of dating in the Scripture for all these events. That is why the dates that we have given must be approximate.

We have generally said that we thought most of these books: Exodus, Leviticus, Numbers, Deuteronomy and Joshua, were written approximately in 1400 BC, but it may be that Joshua was written, as some believe, in 1250–1225 BC. It is all a question of who exactly you believe to be the pharaoh under which Moses led the people of Israel out of Egypt. There is always tremendous division of feelings and opinion in that matter amongst Biblical scholars. However, we do not have to worry quite as much about the date. The point is that it was written and if we say "approximately," we need not worry too much.

The Key to the Book of Joshua

What is the key to the book of Joshua? It seems to me that it is very clearly stated. The key word is undoubtedly *inherit* or *inheritance*. This occurs approximately 58 times in these 24 chapters. It is a word used again and again and again: "to inherit" and "their inheritance.

We have moved in this book from redemption and God's dwelling place to our inheritance. That, I think, we have got to note very clearly. We have moved from redemption, which is something glorious and wonderful. We have also moved from the whole idea of God's dwelling place, (which is His inheritance in the faith) His dwelling place in us and His rights in us. The Lord is after a habitation in us. Now we have moved over to the other side, to our inheritance in the Lord, thinking of our habitation.

This book of Joshua speaks of the inheritance, which Peter tells us is an incorruptible one, something that does not fade away; reserved in heaven for us. I think, really, much of the New

Testament explains this word inheritance. It would be very good if you could look through many of the references to this matter in the New Testament, but wherever we turn in the book of Joshua, we will find everything is related to inheritance. *Everything* is related to inheritance. It does not matter where you turn. All roads lead back to this one thing, inheritance.

Another interesting thing is that redemption, God's dwelling place, and our inheritance are linked together; and not only linked together but are linked together progressively. This simply means that by redemption we are brought to God's habitation, and through being part of God's habitation, we come to our inheritance. There is no inheritance apart from God's habitation. This we must understand very clearly, otherwise we misunderstand the whole message of the letter to the Hebrews, which is not that we can lose our salvation. We cannot lose our salvation, but we can lose our inheritance. It has been expressed very clearly in the book of Revelation that "he that overcometh shall inherit these things" (see Revelation 21:7). Therefore, salvation is not dependent upon overcoming but our inheritance is dependent upon our overcoming.

The book of Joshua tells us very, very clearly that whilst we can be the people of God, we can die in the wilderness. However, we can still be the people of God, still be redeemed, and we can go *over* into the land, we can overcome, and by overcoming can inherit. These two alternatives are always put before every child of God. Do you wish to fall short? You may be a child of God, redeemed by the Lord eternally, but you can fall short and die in the wilderness. Or will you instead go over the Jordan into the land, and in the conflict overcome by God's grace and obtain an inheritance in the land?

We have to recognise then, very clearly, that these three things are linked together: redemption, the habitation of God (God's Church, the Body of the Lord Jesus), and inheritance. These things go together. You have often heard it said, not so much by me but by others, that you will never come to the fulness of Christ individually. We need the Church to obtain the fulness of Christ. We can be individually filled with the Holy Spirit, but we can never come to our part of the *fulness* of Christ except with each other. This is the principle of the Body and the habitation of God. The Lord is far too big to be contained by any one Christian. He needs all the believers together, knit together, fitly framed together, so that He may be expressed and dwell in them all. That is when they become the fulness of Him that filleth all in all.

We ought therefore to note that if the key to the book of Joshua is inheritance, there is another word which is continually stressed throughout this particular book and that is the word *possess*. You will find that word all the way through this book. It simply means that our inheritance has got to be possessed. It does not come to us; we have to possess it. The Lord does not drop it into our laps. We have to go out and possess it. In a wonderful way, salvation comes to us, but we have to possess our inheritance. We go in to possess our inheritance. Whereas God gives us His salvation, and that sovereignly, although we receive it by faith, we can do nothing for it. I cannot struggle for my salvation, as if by struggling greatly I receive it. God gives it to me on the ground that I receive it as a free gift. However, if I am going to know anything of possessing the inheritance, it will often involve a great conflict and a wholly following after the Lord all the days of life.

Another factor that we have got to note is that there is an element of conflict involved with this inheritance—always. It does not matter where you turn, you will always find there is an element of conflict involved with the inheritance. For instance: "*fight* the good fight of faith, lay hold on eternal life, to which thou art called" (see 1 Timothy 6:12). There is always an element of conflict in the very possessing of something to which we have been called.

I think from what I have said, we already have recognised that our inheritance is linked with overcoming and, indeed, that is the book of Joshua. The book of Joshua is simply those that overcame—overcame and sat down. That is the book of Joshua: "He that overcometh will inherit these things."

God's Work

What about the outline of this book? The first thing I want you to notice about the book of Joshua, is how God uses men in His economy. It does not matter what God is doing or when God is moving, it is most interesting to see the way God uses men. God takes men and through men He changes a dispensation. Now, it is so interesting to note this particular turning point in the history of the children of Israel. This story, as someone has said, is really the biography of Joshua. It seems as if it is all Joshua. Although the people themselves did the work, there are many names not even mentioned. Yet, it seems as if Joshua was the one who was used of God to cause them to inherit. Indeed, that is what

God spoke to him in His commission, that He would use Joshua to cause the children of Israel to inherit the land. It is very, very interesting that God never does anything in an organisational or institutional way. That is, it is interesting to note that God always does His work through men, and through them affects the age. Consider Abraham, Joseph, Moses, Joshua, Samuel, and David and so you could go on. It is always men whom God uses.

So, this teaches us one of the most basic and elementary principles in the Bible. God's work is not preaching. It is not meetings. It is not a movement. It is not a teaching. *People* are God's work. We are God's husbandry. We are God's children. We are God's servants. We are the workmanship of God. This is most important for us to realise. The rest flows out of that as we are separated unto the work.

What is this work? It is cooperation with God in the moulding and developing of Christ's character in daily living. If we are just here to promote a movement or someone who is teaching publicly and so on, we are falling very far short. Surely, we are here to edify one another, to build one another up, to cause each other to inherit. I fear that so often we do just the opposite. We cause one another to stumble. We cause friction with one another and then just draw back. There are those people who are all the time being negative, destructive, and so on. Yet, we ought to be people who are causing one another to inherit, provoking one another to love and good works. You can make someone else love—by being lovable. You can make other people do good works by just drawing it out of them instead of being irritable and short and difficult to walk with, just thinking that other people have got to somehow get over it and overcome. This is something we all ought to take note of. God's real work is in us. It is rubbish to talk about the gospel and about the work and about the meeting and about the testimony and to pray and to witness and all of that if something is not being done inside of ourselves. It is the work of God being done. That is the work of God. This is the meaning of the Lord taking up people like Moses and making something out of them and taking up Joshua and making something out of him.

The Conquest of the Land

Then you will find in Joshua a very clear three-fold division. In the first 12 chapters of Joshua, we find the conquest of the land. Then from chapters 13–22 we find the division of the inheritance. Then the last two chapters, chapters 23–24 are the farewell of Joshua. This is the three-fold division, or in some ways a two-fold division except for the conclusion at the end of Joshua's farewell. Many people have said that the first 12 chapters of Joshua are the most woven together package in the whole Bible; you cannot divide them. They are absolutely one whole story, obviously one whole section.

Well, there are one or two things you could note if you turn with me to the first part, the first 12 chapters of Joshua. We find that the first 12 chapters of Joshua are again sub-divided into two. The first five chapters deal with the preparation for the conquest and from 6–12, the last chapters, deal with the actual possession of the land.

What do we find about the preparation for the conquest in the first five chapters? Beginnings are always important, so you find that lessons will come out of there. I might just say this: you will note that God does prepare. (That is the whole point of the book of Numbers—God prepares.) Now there is a new generation that has been tested. They are prepared for three days, and I want you to notice certain things.

The Need to Possess the Land

In the first nine verses, there is the need to possess the land. They need to possess the inheritance. Joshua has told them quite clearly that the Lord has given them everything practically. Yet even though he tells them that it is a very vast area, He says that only the land upon which they tread will they actually possess. He said in verse three, "Every place that the sole of your foot shall tread upon, to you have I given it, as I spake unto Moses." This shows us the need to *possess*, the need to *stand*, and to get over onto the right ground and then to stand, to explore, and to possess it.

You know, some people think that God just says, "You, you, and you. You belong to an inner circle that I am going to take on and make them the chosen ones." But that is not so. Into every child of God's hand has been given all the possibilities of the inheritance. It is up to you as to what you do with them.

For instance, God has given you justification, yet, you want to play around with accusations, and go under them, and mull over them, and get in a mess about them. You feel that you have got such problems in your personality and in your background that are just too big for the Lord. But the Lord has provided you the answer to these problems in the cross! He will get you through if you will only take your possession. It does not matter what it is that you feel can hold you back, God makes provisions. It is up to you to explore them.

The Lord said to Joshua, at the very beginning, "Joshua, it is all yours. Nevertheless, it is only what the soles of your feet tread upon that is yours. All that I promised to your father, Abraham, I will do for you." We need then to possess our inheritance. All the fullness of Christ is ours. God is there then, in our favour, and He will show us the way. He will show us how to stand in the battle, how to fight, how to prepare, how to lay hold. You need to possess it.

The Need to Count the Cost

You will also find in Joshua chapter two that there is the need to count the cost. Many Christians are very clear on consecration and so on, but they have never counted the cost. Now the Lord said that you have got to count the cost. Three times it is reiterated here that you need to count the cost.

First you will find it in Joshua 1:11, "Prepare you victuals; for within three days you are to pass over this Jordan." Then in Joshua 2:16 you find the three days mentioned again. Then in Joshua 3:2, "it came to pass after three days." Joshua made the people wait on the banks of Jordan three whole days and in those three whole days they counted the cost. They sent spies to Jericho to count the cost, just as they had done earlier when they sent twelve spies to count the cost. This time *again* they sent the spies in to count the cost just to see what they were up against and what it was going to cost them to take the land.

Now, you know the Lord has never ever asked anyone to do anything without first sitting down and counting the cost. Many people think they can do things very easily, but they do not count the cost. They do not think about it till after and then they murmur and groan and rebel against the Lord. Yet the Lord would have us sit down and think and recognise and then revisit it. If we are going to inherit the land, we must count the cost. That was very, very necessary. In the possessing of the land of their inheritance they had to count the cost.

The Need of Faith and Obedience

Then the third need I want you to note was the need of faith and obedience and you will find that in chapter two personified in Rahab. Here is someone with whom Biblical scholars have all had great difficulty. When I was first saved, we were always told very dogmatically and categorically that Rahab was not a harlot. She was an innkeeper. There is all the difference in the world between an innkeeper and a harlot, but the whole point is simply this: Rahab was a harlot. You cannot twist the Scriptures to change the meaning. I have great sympathy with the poor Bible scholars, because they find Rahab in the royal line of the Lord Jesus the Messiah. They have felt that it was too vile that a woman of the street could possibly ever be included in the line of the Messiah. But in actual fact, there is no need to cover it up; there is no need to gloss over it. The Scripture quite clearly states it, and the word does not bear the meaning of an innkeeper. Rahab was a woman of the street. On the other hand, we have got to recognise that Jericho was a vile city. It had sunk to the lowest form of depravity and degradation to which any human habitation could sink. In that state, probably Rahab was not *very* much different from the other citizens of Jericho.

However, the Scripture tells us two things or three things in the New Testament about Rahab. First, she is in the royal line of the Messiah. Therefore, we can see she must have married someone who was in the royal line, one of those native of the tribe of Judah. She was obviously married, introduced into the line of the Messiah and became one of the ancestors of the Lord Himself.

Apart from that we see one or two references to her. One is in Hebrews 11:31, saying that she was included with Abraham, Isaac, Jacob, Moses, and all the other great names. Rahab was a woman of faith. Rahab is given to us as an example of faith which means simply that we can be the rockiest type of person in the world, and yet can still become one who shows an example of faith in God. The other thing is that whatever had perverted Rahab and made her what she was, God did something in her because of her faith. James 2:25 says that Rahab was not justified by faith alone but by her works also. What were her works? She took in the messengers and sent them on their way. So, Rahab speaks to us of *faith* and *obedience*, and this is the tremendous need if the land is to be possessed, if we are to gain an inheritance. Do you know that Rahab inherited?

People know a lot about the destruction of all the tribes in the promised land, but they forget that there were people like Rahab who not only risked their lives, and remained alive, but actually inherited their possession in the land. This is something very, very wonderful. I think we should take note of it together. There is the need of faith and obedience.

Deliverance

Then we come to chapters three, four, and five. These three chapters deal with the need of the fundamentals of the cross. If we are then to inherit—if we are going to possess our inheritance, to possess the land, we have not only the need of faith and obedience, but we have got the fundamental need of the cross. I think you can see this is the most foundational thing of all, and you will find it mentioned in two or three forms in these three chapters.

The first thing we come up against when we read chapter three is the Jordan River. What does the Jordan speak to us about? They have already had one crossing of the Red Sea, why did the children of Israel have to cross through another? What is the meaning of it? The Red Sea was a deliverance from Egypt, but the Jordan was a deliverance into the land.

One side of the cross delivers us from our past and from our sin; the other delivers us into all that Christ wants and is. It is not only being half saved. We have been legally saved, our sins have been blotted out, our past has been blotted out, and we have been extricated from this world. Yet, that is only one side of the cross. The other side of the cross is that we should be delivered into the land. The cross not only takes us out of the world, knocks out our past, cuts us off from the whole line of nature—the cross also puts us into Christ, gives us an eternal destiny and vocation, and causes us to inherit it. Jordan therefore speaks of something deeper than the Red Sea.

Crossing the Red Sea was magnificent, it was glorious. Crossing the Jordan was deeper and much, much more positive than the

Red Sea. The Red Sea only got a nation out of Egypt and into the wilderness. The Jordan got them out of the wilderness and into the land. By the opening of the Jordan, God accomplished the end of deliverance. When He brought them out of Egypt, it was to make them a nation in their own land. By the Red Sea, He only did half of it. By the Jordan, He completed it. He brought them into the land.

So, I want you to notice that we have to pass through Jordan if we are going to get into our inheritance. If we are going to possess Christ, if we are going to really know His fullness, it is going to be by a far deeper experience of the cross than ever we knew when first we came to the Lord. Jordan stands for something deeper, something much fuller and more final than even the Red Sea.

The Waters of Jordan

Here, the first thing we note is that the waters of the Jordan are that which divides the wilderness from the promised land. They have got to go over these waters. The way God does it is by putting the ark of His covenant in the centre of the Jordan. When the ark of God's covenant is in the centre of the Jordan, the waters are divided. The Jordan is like dry ground.

This is just where you and I will find the presence of God— in the cross. If you think you are going to find the presence of God anywhere else, consider this: you must remember that the holy anointing oil must never touch the flesh. You will only ever find the presence of God in the cross. It is Christ crucified who is the power of God and the wisdom of God. So, we have to recognise firstly that the Jordan is the natural barrier between the wilderness as such and the promised land into which God was taking them. They had to pass that Jordan to take them over.

Memorial Stones

The second thing I want you to notice is that in these chapters there are memorial stones of which a lot is made. I think it would help you to have a description. It would just seem that God was asking Joshua to take twelve men, one to represent each of the tribes, to go to where the priests were standing with the ark in the centre of the Jordan, and to take twelve large stones and place them on the promised land side of the Jordan. Yet when you read more carefully, you will notice that not only did that actually happen—twelve men were chosen to go back to where the ark was in the midst of the Jordan, and take twelve large stones out from the midst of the river and place them on the promised land side— but you also find that Joshua took twelve stones from the other side of the Jordan and planted them in the bed of the river.

What does this mean? It speaks simply of this: that one nature, one life, one kind of person has been buried in the Jordan. An altogether new person has been raised. This is just what baptism symbolises. We are buried with Christ in baptism, and we are raised with Him to walk in a newness of life. If we are going to possess our inheritance it will be only as we understand what it is to have been crucified with Christ. Twelve stones were buried, and the waters drowned them. Twelve new stones are set in place as a memorial and as a testimony to the grace and sovereignty of God of the new life—new beginning. So let us understand the meaning of that. God is finished with one kind of person. God took forty years to finish with that generation—till they died—that ended it. Now, He has got a new nation and a new people and these stones are the memorial of that.

Circumcision

Again, you will notice another thing in these chapters—they are all circumcised. This speaks of the cross and our affection. This speaks of the cross and our natural life. It is not simply enough to know generally that our old nature has been crucified, but now we have before us the circumcision of our natural life. It is something which is really put away and dealt with. So, you see this is something which is very full, very complete.

Then, we find they call the name of that place Gilgal which means *a wheel* or *rolling* because it says in Joshua 5:9, "And the Lord said to Joshua, 'Today I have rolled away the reproach of Egypt from you.'" So, the name of that place to this day is called *Gilgal* (which sounds like the Hebrew word for *to roll*). This was the first place they put their feet in the promised land. There they stood up twelve great stones, rather like Stonehenge and they called that place *Gilgal*. It was from that day forward always called Gilgal. The wheel.

Now what is God speaking about? He says, "I have rolled off the reproach of Egypt from you." How has God rolled off the reproach of Egypt? They are forty years distant from Egypt! Surely there is no reproach of Egypt upon them. What is this wheel? Listen. The cross is a wheel. It takes you right round the whole circle of your life and brings you back to nothing. That is exactly what happens among them. They went right round everything till every part of their natural life was exhausted, until they died. Then the Lord said, "I've rolled off the reproach of Egypt."

It is finished. Egypt is no longer in them. We have often been told that God took them out of Egypt, but it took forty years for God to take Egypt out of them. This was the reproach of Egypt that God rolled off by a circuit, by a full wheel, by a full cycle. Some of us have to travel sometimes a full cycle in experience when God deals with us by the cross. Do let us understand something of that when we come back to something and frustratedly say, "Why wasn't this at the beginning?"

Then suddenly you find they all sit down and they celebrate the Passover. Why didn't they celebrate the Passover at the beginning? It is because when God has taken us the full cycle of our natural life, we need to be re-established in what it means to be justified. If we do not know what it is for Christ who has been offered for us—*for us*, for our sins to be washed away—God could never really deal with our sins. To really deal with our old nature means we have got to be firmly grounded in the fact that we have been justified by the grace of God. Otherwise, I am afraid we end up introverted. We end up so messed up the enemy can do anything with us. We have got to understand what it is that Christ died *for* us.

So, then the Lord has shown them something of the meaning of the Jordan when He has taught them of the full cycle, when He has taken them around, and rolled off this reproach of Egypt. They have seen what it is to have been drowned in the river and for the new stone and the testimony of God's new creation to be raised on the banks. He has circumcised them afresh to renew His covenant with the new man and new creation, His circumcision is just a mark. Then God says, "Now sit down and celebrate the Passover."

You see, here you have a very full picture of the need of the cross. If we are going to inherit the inheritance, the cross has got to do its work. Otherwise, we will all be evading the issue. There are many people who can only hold onto their peace by evading issues. They are frightened to face the Lord fully. They are frightened to face issues fully. There are things that they just dare not, dare not think about. You all know people who take it out on one another because they find that they are facing the issue when they look at you. This is something which only the Lord can deal with, and He has to deal with it by the cross. If we are going to inherit, it is going to be by the cross.

In the last few verses of chapter five (vs. 13–15), you will find that Joshua has a very vivid experience. He was outside the walls of Jericho and suddenly he sees a Man, a Man of war obviously, with a great sword in His hand. He is standing with His sword unsheathed, obviously He is going to execute. Joshua immediately asked Him who He is. Is He for them or is He against them? He replied, "Neither." That is very interesting. You would have thought He would have said that He was with them. Instead, He said "Neither. I am Captain of the Lord's host." This tells us the need of the headship of Christ. If we are always expecting (as so often we are) that the Lord will be with us, taking our side, I think we are going to have, at some time or another, another thing coming. The Lord does not take our side. When the Lord says, "I will not fail you," it is only insofar as you are with the Lord. It is when you are wholly *with the Lord*, that the Lord does not fail you. He does not take your side. As soon as you take sides, the Lord leaves you to fight it out. As soon as you take the Lord's side, the Lord Himself is your protection. The thing that Joshua had to learn was that he was not the leader of the people. This One was Captain of the Lord's host, and He was come to lead them into victory.

So, we must learn these things if we are going to inherit. There is not only the fundamental need of the cross, but the Holy Spirit has got to really lead us. We have got to be absolutely under the captaincy of the Holy Spirit—otherwise we get nowhere. We can never be under the Lordship of Christ unless we know the cross. We can pretend we are, but sooner or later our façade will be seen through. The cross is the only means by which we can really be brought under the Lordship of Christ. Therefore, you see that their preparation for the land is rather amazing. It is something which, as far as they are concerned, is full of principle.

Possessing the Land

Now the possession of the land is something on which we will not take so long because it is self-explanatory. I do not know whether most of you know that Joshua has been called one of the most brilliant generals in history. In fact, there was once a series of articles in the *Evening Standard* on Joshua and others as military commanders written by a military man himself. Joshua has been hailed as one of the most brilliant generals in history. Certainly, when you read through the book of Joshua you see that he knew exactly what he was doing in the way in which at one point he used this form of attack and then he always changed to another form. He never used the same form twice. Under the leadership of the Lord, Joshua was continually changing. He was always surprising. You could see that it was because he was surprising that he won the victory so often. It says again and again through Joshua, "... he came upon them unawares." In one place it tells you why he came upon them unawares. It was because they didn't sleep all night. They journeyed all through the night. That was how they came upon their enemy when they least expected it.

Yet perhaps the most remarkable thing of all, as far as Joshua was concerned, was that the whole of the promised land was split up into a very large number of petty kingdoms (none of which was in any way really allied to the other). There were a whole lot of little kingdoms—Amorite kingdoms, Hittite kingdoms, and so on—little groups all through the land. The whole thing was split up into these little kingdoms. They were only allied in one thing—against the threat of a common invasion. When that came, they all had an alliance which they invoked, and which meant that they were all united against one common invader.

Now, the Lord told them to cross over a river against Jericho at Gilgal. In a way, this is very wonderful because Joshua did not lead the children of Israel to attack the land from the South. If he had done so, he would have met with a very strong range of fortresses which were built right across the southernmost parts of these kingdoms, and which for quite some time had been manned against the Egyptian invasion. If they had fought to take the land from the South, they would have had a very, very stiff fight indeed. Neither did they take the land by coming down from the North because Joshua knew (and the Lord knew better than Joshua) that if they came down by the North, all the kingdoms would unite in one solid block. Instead, they came over the Jordan the one way that the tribes thought was impossible, particularly because the Jordan was in flood tide. The banks had been overflowed on either side to make it absolutely impossible to take over a whole nation of people. So, you see, that is why they were not really so very afraid on this side as they watched the children of Israel encamping on the other side of the Jordan. But it was that strategy of Joshua's that so wonderfully proved itself in the end because he did one simple thing. When the Lord took them over the Jordan, they attacked Jericho and then they attacked Ai. These two cities were absolute keys to their victory. These cities guarded the passes into central Palestine. If they could take these two cities, the whole of central Palestine would open. Joshua's strategy was to take the whole of central Palestine and cut the land into two portions.

The next part of the book of Joshua, from chapters 6–12, is the story of the campaign of Joshua. From chapters 6–8 you have the story of his central campaign, that is, Jericho, Ai, and then Gibeon, which was all open. He took that very easily in a sense. Then all the kingdoms of the South banded together in an alliance. Five kings particularly banded together and attacked the Gibeonites. Joshua slaughtered them all and then went on for the conquest of the whole south of the land. Then the kingdoms of the North, who were thought to be stronger, allied themselves and they attacked Joshua. Hazor was the man who actually was the leader of them at the place called Merom, at the waters of Merom. There, the final battle for the land was fought and the whole of the North was taken.

I think you will all know some stories from the campaigns of Joshua. You all know the story of Jericho, for instance. For six days they marched around Jericho, the priests first, the ark next, and then the people in orderly fashion—silently without a single word or murmur of conversation, only the trumpets blowing.

Then on the seventh day, the Sabbath, they went around six times like that. But on the seventh time, when the trumpets blew, the people shouted and the walls fell down. You know, I think something of the spiritual significance of that story surely is timing—which is important in all God's victories—you may have to wait seven days and on the seventh day you may have to wait a very long time, but God's victories are always timed. That needs faith. To put the priests first and to blow the trumpets needed a lot of faith. To shout on the seventh day on the seventh round and then to expect to see the walls fall down; just to shout was certainly expecting. This was quite an amount of faith.

So, from chapters 6–8 you have got his central campaign, from chapter 9–10 you have got his southern campaign, and chapter 11 deals with his northern campaign. Then chapter 12 is the summing up of the lot. These chapters, chapters 6–12, tell the story of the campaigns of Joshua.

2.
Joshua Study Guide

Introduction

Joshua is the first book in the second section of the Bible called in the Hebrew Canon *The Prophets*, and in the Greek *The Historical Books*. The Prophets were subdivided into two—*The Former Prophets* and *The Latter Prophets*. *The Former Prophets* comprise four books—Joshua, Judges, Samuel and Kings, and *The Latter Prophets* also comprise four books—Isaiah, Jeremiah, Ezekiel and *The Twelve*. *The Historical Books* comprises 12 books, Joshua to Esther, and cover approximately 1000 years of history.

We see in this period of history three great phases:

1. Moses to Samuel
2. Samuel to the division of the Kingdom into Judea and Israel
3. The division of the Kingdom to Malachi

We need also to remember:

a) The Pentateuch is the foundation. The Historical section is the building, founded upon the principles laid down in the Pentateuch. Indeed all those principles are illustrated positively or negatively in this section.

b) There is, of course, also much history in the Pentateuch, and we must not take the title "historical books" as if this is the only history in the Old Testament. It is a somewhat loose title. In many ways the Hebrew title "The Prophets" comes much nearer to the heart of the matter. It is not the history as we know generally. For instance, much is excluded, and much included according to the aim. Once again, the aim governs the scope. It is, in fact, history but it is history prophetically interpreted. It is history from God's standpoint, as and how it affects and realises divine ends.

c) It is worth noting that the connection between the Pentateuch and Joshua is particularly strong.

Authorship and Date

It would seem, in many parts of the book, that *Joshua* was written by an eye-witness or by someone living near to that time—e.g. "we," "us," etc., and "unto this day." See Joshua 4:9; 5:1, 6, and 9; 6:25; 7:26; 8:28–29; 9:27; 10:27; 15:63; etc.

The Talmud asserts that Joshua was the author of Deuteronomy 34:5–12 as well as the book of Joshua. The one piece of internal evidence is Joshua 24:26. On the whole, Jewish tradition therefore accepts the authorship of Joshua himself, with additions and editing by later scribes. Some scholars think that *Joshua* in its present form was the work of Samuel. Whoever it was, the main body of the book must have been written very shortly after the main events described, if not during them. It appears, therefore, that there is much to support the view that if Joshua did not write this book, he certainly supplied the material for it.

The book covers a period of 25 years and can be dated approximately 1400 BC although there is controversy over this date.

The man Joshua was an Ephraimite (1 Chronicles 7:27), his original name being Hoshea (Jesus, meaning *The Lord is Salvation*). He led the army against Amalek (Exodus 17:10) and was Moses' personal attendant (Exodus 24:13; 33:11). He was one of the twelve spies (Numbers 14:6–9, 30, and 38). Josephus says that Joshua was 85 years of age when he succeeded Moses, and we know that he died at the age of 110 years (Joshua 24:29). His name appears in the Tel El Amarna Tablets, 614 BC. He has been favourably compared with the greatest military commanders of history.

Key to the Book

The key is undoubtedly the word *inherit* or *inheritance*. It is used approximately 58 times.

In Joshua, we find ourselves having moved from redemption and God's dwelling place, to our inheritance, although all of these are intimately and progressively linked together. Everywhere we turn in this book, we are led to the matter of inheritance.

Thus we ought to note that the word *possess* is frequently used. Our inheritance has to be possessed. Another factor we ought to note is that there is a very big element of conflict associated with possessing. Indeed, inheriting is always linked in the Bible with overcoming. This is Joshua.

Outline of the Book

Note the importance of men in God's economy. For example Abraham, Moses, etc. God's work is supremely "men." He is not interested in "things" but in "people." We see this in the man Joshua. This book, dealing with one of the great moves forward in God's plan, begins with Joshua's call and commission and ends with his home call. We must never lose sight of this tremendous truth.

In Joshua we find a clear three-fold division:

I. The Conquest of the Land: Joshua 1–12

II. The Division of the Inheritance: Joshua 13–22

III. The Farewell of Joshua: Joshua 23–24

I. The Conquest of the Land

A. The preparation for the conquest: Joshua 1–5

i. The need to possess. See Joshua 1:3, 5, 6, and 11. What has been given and provided, must be possessed.

ii. The need to count the cost. See Joshua 2. The spies had to face the realities in faith. (Note also *3 days–Calvary*. See Joshua 1:11; 2:16; 3:2)

There is a cost to overcoming. Our Saviour has paid it, but we must also lay down our lives.

iii. The need of faith and obedience. Note the Jordan was in full harvest flood tide. Naturally impossible to pass. Rahab is also a most remarkable example of this faith and obedience.

iv. The fundamental need of the cross: Joshua 3–5

a. Jordan and the Red Sea.

Christ's death for us as pictured in the Red Sea.

Christ death as us as pictured in the Jordan.

b. The memorial stones. Twelve stones were buried in the river and twelve were set up on the bank of the promised land. Note in Joshua 3:16 that the water was cut off at the city called Adam. The old Adam is crucified with Christ.

c. Circumcision

d. Gilgal–*Rolling, wheel* see Joshua 5:9

e. The Passover

v. The need of the leadership of Christ by the Holy Spirit. See Joshua 5:13–15. Joshua (Jesus) is a type of Christ, and the Captain of the Lord's host, a type of the Holy Spirit. Note also the "ark" etc. there is no other way of knowing the Lordship of Christ but by the Spirit.

B. The possession of the land: Joshua 6–12

Joshua has been called a brilliant general. The land was divided into quite a number of petty kingdoms, not at all united, except against common invasion. Joshua did not attack the South (it was well fortified), nor did he attack from the North (this would have united all against him). He attacked across the Jordan when it was in harvest floodtide, thus splitting the country in two. Jericho and Ai were absolutely essential to victory, as they dominated the passages into the land.

i. The Central Campaign: Joshua 6–8

a.   Jericho: see Joshua 6. Note the timing, the perseverance, faith, praise and "soles of their feet"

b.   Achan's sin: see Joshua 7. Note the things taken, stolen, deceitfully hidden; it had to be judged and put away.

c.   Ai: see Joshua 8:1–29. Note that sin had to be dealt with before victory; all the people had to be involved.

d.   The Altar built: Joshua 8:30–35. Christ's work on the Cross is the basis for all overcoming.

ii. The Southern campaign: Joshua 9–10

a.   The alliance of the Canaanite tribes: Joshua 9:1–2. Note the alliance of evil directed against the people of God possessing their possessions.

b.   The cleverness of the Gibeonites: Joshua 9:3–27. Note the Satanic devices in the matter of overcoming. Once confessed, God turned the tables on Satan.

c.   The defeat of the five kings: Joshua 10:1–28. Note the need of executive action, "feet on their necks."

d.   The conquest of the rest of the South: Joshua 10:29–43

iii. The Northern Campain: Joshua 11

All was taken by faith. Note what Joshua did not overcome. See Joshua 11:13, 22

iv. Summary of the whole: Joshua 12

II. The Division of the Inheritance: Joshua 13–22

A. Introduction and the 2 ½ tribes' inheritance: Joshua 13

B. Judah's inheritance: Joshua 14–15

Note:

1. Caleb's inheritance–Hebron: Joshua 14:1–15

2. The part played by Othniel: Joshua 15:13–19

C. Joseph's inheritance: Joshua 16–17

D. The seven remaining tribes: Joshua 18–19

Note how faithfully the chronicler mentions whether they fully drove out the enemy or not. See Joshua 15:63, 16:10; 17:12, 13 cf. 18

E. Refuge cities and Levitical cities, Joshua 20:21

Note:

1. Cities of refuge. See Joshua 20

2. Levitical cities. See Joshua 21. There are 48 cities in all, including 6 cities of refuge and 13 priestly cities

3. The Levites' portion throughout this book, e.g. Joshua 13:14 and 33; 14:3–4; 18:7

F. Warning to the 2 ½ tribes in Joshua 22

1. Their position on the fringe. This is always dangerous.

2. The Altar: Christ crucified, our oneness, our unifying bond.

III. The Farewell of Joshua. Joshua 23–24

A. The farewell, Joshua 23:1–24:15

B. The renewal of the Covenant, Joshua 24:16–28

C. The death of Joshua, Joshua 24:29–31

D. The burial of Joseph's bones and Eleazer, Aaron's son. Joshua 24:29–33

Message of the Book

In many vital ways, Joshua is the consummation of Exodus. Our redemption has two sides, "out of ... into," Exodus 6:6–8. The believer is brought out of "Egypt" by faith in the blood of the Lamb, and he is brought into "the promised land," by the power of the Holy Spirit. The finished work of Christ is sufficient to bring us out of one world or realm and into the new. Nevertheless, to possess what God has so freely given us we need to know that the Cross and the Spirit is now our experience. "Moses, My servant is dead ..." The Law can never bring us into the fullness of Christ, but in the book of Joshua we are shown the principles by which the spiritual inheritance is possessed. Note then the following principles:

1. Our inheritance will not just come to us. It must be possessed by faith and obedience.

2. We can settle at any given point and that will be the measure of our inheriting.

3. Conflict is involved, not only in the possessing of our inheritance, but in a heavenly position.

4. Three things are essential:

    i. to be absolutely and utterly devoted

    ii. a deep working of the cross

    iii. the leadership of the Holy Spirit

5. The Lord alone is able to cause us to inherit. His Word is continually, "I will not fail thee, nor forsake thee. Be strong and of good courage ... Be not afraid, neither be thou dismayed, for the Lord thy God is with thee whithersoever thou goes" (Joshua 1:5, 6, 9.) We are well able to possess our inheritance because the Lord is with us.

Recommended Books:

The Foundations of Bible History: Joshua, Judges - John Garstang
Gleanings in Joshua - A.W. Pink
Joshua & the Land of Promise - F.B. Meyer
Israel in Canaan under Joshua & the Judges - A. Edersheim

Questions

1. What are the key words in the book of Joshua?

2. Describe three outstanding miracles recorded in Joshua. What spiritual application can you find for the Christian life today?

3. Give the names of two outstanding examples of faith in Joshua, apart from Joshua himself.

4. Give two examples of warnings given to us in Joshua.

5. What is the greatest warning given to us in chapter 9?

6. Why is there so much mention of "conflict" in the book?

7. Give examples of "absolute utterness" found in these chapters: Joshua 8, 10, 14, 22, 24

8. What is so special about the Levites' inheritance?

9. What examples of the Cross can you find in chapters 3–5?

10. Read chapters 23–24. State briefly what you learn about the faithfulness and power of God from these chapters.

11. What do you learn about the attitude of the 2 ½ tribes toward the eternal purpose of God in their choice of an inheritance (see Joshua 13:8–32 and Numbers 32)?

12. What have you learned about the Holy Spirit from the book of Joshua?

3.
Judges

To begin this study on Judges we will read part of chapter two, the one little phrase that is reiterated over and over again: "And so-and-so drove not out the Canaanites" or "other inhabitants." We find it again and again in the first chapter, and then in chapter two, verse three . We now come to the seventh book of the Bible, the second book of the historical section or the historical books of the Old Testament. I suppose we come to a book that is very rarely studied. I do not know how many, even of those who are older amongst you, have really studied the book of Judges. It seems that this book is relegated to the Sunday school, where most Christians seem to have heard the stories that are in it. It is a vivid book, vivid in every way. In some ways, it is quite crude. It has, I suppose, stories that hardly any other part of the Bible have—stories of brutality, of crudity, and of much else. Yet, this book of Judges is one that is very, very important indeed, and in its own way, it is quite as important as the book of Joshua. You see, since we have come to this book, we have to deal with some rather unpleasant things. However, I think we shall find that as we go through it, we are going to learn something of the meaning the Lord had for including this in the Word.

Of course, you can see straightaway that Judges has been written by someone else. All the other six books have had their own stamp: the first five have a certain character about them, which we have noticed. Joshua also has a character, but this book of Judges is quite remarkable. I have been quite surprised myself when I find things like Samson saying that he was "quits with the Philistines." [see the *JPS Tanakh* 1917 version of Judges 15:3, which in other versions is written as: "I shall be blameless"]. I never thought I would find that expression in the Bible. I never thought I would find that the men of a certain place were left-handed and could sling a stone within a hairbreadth and never miss, and other little colloquial, almost slang phrases like, "You have ploughed with my heifer, and therefore you have solved my riddle," referring to his wife. You see, this book has a stamp about it, which immediately reveals that we are in new territory.

The Cycle

The other thing about Judges that I want you to note, straightaway, is the almost complete contrast between it and Joshua. As you know, Joshua is a book of victory. *The* element in the book of Joshua is overcoming—"and they overcame." Whilst it now and again underlines the fact that certain parts of the tribe who they should have driven out were not driven out, its real emphasis is an overcoming by the people of God and the possession of their inheritance. But Judges is a book full of the opposite. It is a book of declension. It is a book of defection. It is a book of division. It is a book of depravity. It is a book of every kind of disorder. From beginning to end, Judges is a book that deals with the seamy side of the Christian experience. It is something that many people do not like. Just in the way that they love Ephesians, but do not like Corinthians, so they love Joshua, but do not love Judges. But, you see, Corinthians is of necessity the other side of Ephesians—it is the earthly side, the earthly aspect of the heavenly. Judges is the earthly aspect of the other side of overcoming. It reveals to us something of the flesh and blood warfare that we are really in if we mean business with the Lord.

We find that Judges is not only a book of disorder and division, defeat, and so on, but it is also a book of repentance and deliverance. Continually through this book, we are finding that the Lord's children are being brought back to the place of repentance and then the Lord delivers them. We almost grow weary as we read through the story of, "then the children of Israel sought the Lord and their cry came up unto the Lord, and He raised up a saviour for them," or "a deliverer for them," and so on. Then we get the story of their deliverance.

Nevertheless, the book of Judges is really a cycle, a very wearying cycle with very little real progress. If we include the book of Ruth in it, we find that we have real progress. If we leave out the book of Ruth, we have very little progress in this book. For instance, we find that the people sin, they follow after foreign gods, they devote themselves to foreign gods, they intermarry, then they become slaves to some tribe or nation, then when they cry unto the Lord, the Lord raises them up a deliverer, then they are delivered. Within a few years, we find that they have a 40 years' rest or 40 years' peace, and then suddenly, the next phrase is, "Then the children of Israel joined themselves again to other gods." There seems to be very little progress at all until once again, the Lord raises up another deliverer, and once again, the people are delivered, and once again, there is a period of rest.

It is very interesting that the periods of rest are far longer than the periods of captivity. So that really, in a sense, (and we must remember this) the Holy Spirit is focusing attention upon the failure and not upon the going on. In this particular book, we find that the focus is not on the far much greater amount of peace that there was when they followed after the Lord, but the attention is focused continually upon the decline and declension, and the coming back once again to the same trouble. It is a cycle. That is why many people find the book of Judges so wearing; they begin to hear, then they go right the way round, and they come back to zero and then they start all over again and come back. Really, 12 times this happened in all the lives of these 12 judges and you have got this cycle. You have 12 judges and therefore you have got the 12 cycles or revolutions, again and again, through this particular phase of history. It is therefore something very wearing.

God's Faithfulness and Mercy

Then again, I want you to notice that even if there is all this failure, the thing that does shine out in the book of Judges is the faithfulness and the mercy of God. He never gives up His people. This should be a tremendous comfort to us. We can commit the most gross sins; we can get into a place where we are far away from the Lord because of our own doing, and yet the Lord refuses to give up His people. He refuses! The Lord will remain in the plan until the last vestige is destroyed. Then He will raise up His children, if necessary, from the stones (see Matthew 3:9). But the Lord will not forsake His inheritance. He will not forsake the land. He will not forsake His people. Everything can go. Everything can be perverted. Everything can be compromised, but the Lord refuses to forsake His people. This is the most wonderful message of the book of Judges.

As far as the people go, in the revelation of God's purpose in the Bible, the book of Judges is a serious break in step. As far as history goes, the book itself is just a story of a cruel cycle. But in God's revealing of His purpose to us, Judges speaks simply of this: for the first time, authority is underlined and emphasised. Up to now, we have had much else revealed to us. We have had the beginnings of all God's thoughts. His great sovereignty has reached out through individuals to get what He is after. Then a people are redeemed and His dwelling place is revealed. Then how we can become part of His dwelling place is shown to us in Leviticus. Then probation, and responsibility shown as an essential characteristic of being made part of God's habitation. After that He shows love as the basis for all this. The one thing that the Lord looks for more than anything is the heart that is really in love with Him. Then the book of Joshua tells us how we must go over into the land to possess our inheritance. It is not merely the Lord's inheritance in us, that is His habitation, but our inheritance in the Lord that is the fullness of the Lord Jesus. These two things are brought together.

Now, we find that this book of Judges is going to underline for us this whole question of authority. In other words, Judges is a preparatory book. That is why so many of the early church fathers always felt that Ruth and Judges were part of the same work, and why even now most people do believe that Ruth and Judges were written by the same author. It is a preparatory movement, as it were, to prepare us for the king. These two books prepare and condition our hearts and minds for the whole concept of kingship. Judges, on the one side, is showing us by lack, by the very lack of authority, the need for kingship. Ruth is showing us on the other side how God, in the midst of the lack, is working to get to His end, which is His house and throne in Israel.

When we have these two books together, we have two preparatory books in God's revelation of His whole purpose. We have seen something of His house, we have seen something of our inheritance. Now, going forth, the whole of the Bible is a progressive revelation. It begins with great themes and then begins to develop details. We have begun with the great themes of the Bible. Authority is not so much, I think, a theme; it is something that is part of a great theme. In other words, God's habitation is a great theme; authority is one of the elementary characteristics of His habitation. So now we come really to see this in the book of Judges.

Authorship and Date

What about the authorship and the date of this book? The first thing I would like to say is that no one knows the author. No name is given. No hint is given and therefore there has been wild speculation. Some say this book was written during the time of King Josiah and his great reformation. Others believe that it was written much earlier and that it could not possibly have been in the time of King Josiah. The rabbis always taught that Samuel was the author of Judges, and certainly, it would seem that Judges, Ruth, and the first part of Samuel are linked as a continuous work. You would have to read for yourself those three books and judge as to whether you feel that is so. But the Jewish rabbis always claimed that it was the work of Samuel, as also was Ruth, and as also was the first part of the book of Samuel.

The book of Judges was written somewhere between 1400 BC and 1000 BC. It covers roughly 300 years—to be more precise, 330 years. We can say with real certainty that this book covers approximately 300 years of history from Joshua to Eli. That is quite a big span, from Joshua right over to Eli, for the coming of Samuel the prophet. This is why many believe it is Samuel who has written it as a preparatory movement to kingship. You must remember that Samuel was God's instrument for bringing in kingship. He undoubtedly was God's instrument. His whole life was bound up with the house of God and the throne. I believe that Samuel saw the throne as a means for the house. Therefore, his work has been, as you can see, a preparatory work and then the actual description of the coming monarchy—first the false one, and then the real one.

It is interesting that some scholars feel that David may have, in his very early days, learned from Samuel something of God's intention regarding His house. He first found, not only from his father, who was of course by tradition one of the weavers of the veil in the tabernacle, but he may well have learned from Samuel something of God's intention regarding His house. It may have been that Samuel was the one who instilled in David such a love for the house of God.

Another thing that we should remember is that this book is not consecutive, necessarily. This is where many people make a big mistake in the book of Judges. They think that all these Judges are consecutive. If you look at a map, you will find that far from being consecutive, many of these Judges may have been contemporary. For instance, Othniel judged in the south. Gideon judged in central Palestine. Deborah and Barak were in the north. Then, Jephthah was in Gilead east of the Jordan. Then you have Samson in the far south where the Philistines were. There were also many others. Shamgar is the only one who we do not know exactly where he judged. The point is simply that the judges may not necessarily have been consecutive. There may be quite a bit of overlapping, and in some cases, they may have been judging contemporaneously with each other. So, there is no real difficulty in that.

Another point that you ought to remember is this: Judges chapters 17–21 are definitely not in their chronological order. They are an appendix to the story of the deliverances of God through these judges. The first is a story of Micah the Ephraimite and the second is the story of the wickedness of the men of Gibeah. Ruth, we believe is the third part of that appendix. It is the story of a couple who went from their native land, Bethlehem Ephrathah, to live in Moab, and all that happened to them. All these three narratives at the end of the book of Judges can be dated at the beginning of this period. For instance, you will note that in the story of the terrible wickedness and depravity of the men of Gibeah, Phinehas was still alive. This means that it must have been at the very beginning, probably in the lifetime of Othniel. Then again, we think that the story of Ruth was very early in the record. So, it is likely that the only part that we can call history in a more chronological order is from Judges chapters 3–16 . The last part is the appendix and the first part is an introduction. That, I think we do have to note. I think most of you will agree if you read the book of Ruth, (it is only four chapters and it is a very easy story to read) that it follows quite normally onto the end of Judges. It is the sovereignty of God that the Holy Spirit has placed it here in the Bible.

God's Purpose for Israel in the Time of the Judges

What is the key to the book of Judges? I think we ought to take note of the three reasons that the writer gives for this phase of Israel's history. They are found in chapter two and chapter three. He gives three reasons for this phase in Israel's history. The first is in Judges 2:20–23: to visit the disobedience of the children of Israel. The second is in Judges 3:4: to prove the children of Israel as to what was really in their heart. The third reason is in Judges 3:2: to teach them to war. These were the three reasons that whoever wrote Judges gave for this account. First, to visit the disobedience of the children of Israel with punishment, secondly, to prove the new generation as to what was in their heart, and thirdly, to teach them to war. I think these three things teach us something about the Lord.

To Visit the Disobedience of the Children of Israel

The Lord always chastens those He loves. We never get away with anything. If as children of God, we do something, we may not have to pay the penalty, but we will be chastened, and we will learn by our chastening. "Before I was afflicted, I went astray" (see Psalm 119:67). The Lord afflicts us and then reins us in. That is why it is often so tragic to see children of God who are disobeying the Lord or leaving issues unsettled with the Lord because the only way the Lord can really establish us is by chastening and by affliction. He shaves us of so much of our waywardness and fashions us in a new way.

To Prove What was in Their Hearts

The second thing is that the Lord is always proving us. I bet you have noticed that. He led them through the wilderness to prove them, to find out what was in their hearts. He is always proving. I bet you have noticed how the Lord has always got things on probation. Always, always, always, the Lord is proving, proving, proving. He puts us into situations and puts us into trials, all to prove us, just to find out what ground is in our hearts. This, I think, is something very interesting. However, the thing that I think we should dwell on is this: if the Lord visits our disobedience and leads us this way to prove us, He leaves thorns in our side to prove us. He will teach us through our failures and weaknesses. This is one of the most wonderful things: He teaches us even through our failures. This is the most amazing thing.

To Teach Them to War

He makes us men and women of war. Why does the Lord allow this? It is partly because it was the only way He could teach His people. It was the only way He could teach them. It was the only way He could prove them and instruct them. He had to teach them to war. They did not know war. The other generation, now grown up, had forgotten what war was like and they had to learn about it.

So, I think we, together, have to learn just how the Lord does lead us in our ways. Some people seem to be so terribly upset when they have made a mistake of the smallest kind. They seem to think the Lord is going to cut them out altogether, but in actual fact, your mistakes are often woven into the Lord's way for you. You may not know it, but there is nothing, not a single thing in this whole universe, including Satan and the whole of hell that can do anything to you but increase you [in Christ]. When we get hold of this, it changes everything. When we view this history through a magnifying glass, we find that the Lord is just simply proving everything. He is bringing everything under judgement, and He is exposing all the weakness that is in His people.

When we take the overall picture from end to end, we find that the Lord is steadily working through His people. This is why Paul says to the Corinthians, "there must needs be factions and divisions amongst you that those who are approved may be made manifest" (see 1 Corinthians 11:19). Factions and divisions can only bring out what is of God and can only expose what is not in the people. In the same way, a thorn in the flesh, as Paul had, can only bring out the beauty and the loveliness and the strength of Christ in a believer. That is all it can do. If there is anything else, if we can be offended in the Lord by these things, we will go under, and we shall be exposed as having compromised, mixed motives in our hearts. So, let us learn simply from this that the Lord is teaching us through these very things to be men and women of war—in the right way hardened.

God's Purpose in the Failure of Men

You see then that this book has a lot to do with deliverances. It is a book of deliverance. Indeed, the Hebrew word that we have translated for us as "judges" is the word "deliver," or "deliverance," or "saviour." It can mean a magistrate. In one sense it can mean "a ruler" and in another, it can be "a deliverer." Or it can mean "a saviour" in another. Here then is the story of man's failure and over against that is the salvation of God. It is man's failure and God's deliverances all the way through. It is a record of failure which is leading to deliverance. Every time, failure leads to deliverance. The majority may fail, but it leads to those who will serve the Lord with their whole heart; we see that in every situation the Lord has got His man. Whether it is a man that we know nothing about like Shamgar who slew so many with an ox goad, or a man like Abdon that we know very little about, or a man like Jephthah who was a little foolish, or Samson who was so weak in many ways, or whether it was a man like Gideon who is so noble and yet he failed. In all these cases, the Lord has got His man who may fail, but He has His man.

These are the ones who really wanted to follow the Lord. Quite a number of those mentioned in this book are found in the record of those who through faith overcame[1]. Samson is there in spite of his life, Barak is there, Jepthath is there in spite of his terrible mistake, and you will find that many of them are there.

I want you also to note that the Lord takes the very defeat of His people and brings it to victory. Through this very means, He instructs His people in the essentials for overcoming. I think we ought to recognise that and see that in the midst of a terrible story of decline and division, there is the beautiful story of Ruth. That is just how the Lord always seems to work. Everything else may be corrupt and perverted but here at the heart of it, there is one of the most beautiful stories in the Bible. Absolutely pure. Crystal clear in the very heart of this awful, awful history, here we find the Lord is working His purpose in it. It may be that everything else around us has collapsed, everything else may have gone awry, but the Lord has got, as it were, His own one, on whom and in whom He is working and really moving through to His end.

Causes and Effects

Another thing I wanted to note about this book is not only that it is about failure and deliverance, but it is a book of causes and effects. Gideon took a concubine and had a son, Abimelech. This is just one small phrase but a whole chapter is taken up with the effect of how Abimelech destroyed his 70 brothers, destroyed the lot of them. One small mistake after victory and the effect is tremendous. A whole royal people, a whole seed was wiped out except for one man who escaped.

1 See Hebrews 11

So, we find in this book that all the way through it is cause and effect. Samson was a mighty man. We are told where his strength lay, and then we are told how he let the secret out. We are told how he lost the mark of his strength and how this ended with his eyes being put out.

Throughout this book, in big things and in small things there is cause and effect. The first chapter keeps on saying, "and Benjamin drove not out the Canaanites, and Naphtali drove not out so-and-so, and Asher drove not out so-and-so." Through the book, we find that these people who they did not drive out had now become powerful and strong in the midst of the people of God and they took over and overwhelmed the people of God. All the way through this book there is cause and there is the effect. This can be traced out in our spiritual life with the Lord. How the Lord continually, if we are open to Him, traces the effects of causes in our lives. How often when someone collapses suddenly or goes out suddenly, you find that there is a cause that the Holy Spirit has got to address before it can be recovered.

The Key to Judges—Authority

In spite of all this about cause and effect, about failure and deliverance, the key to this book is something else. It is contained in the phrase that is repeated again and again in the appendix. It is not repeated in any other part of the book. In Judges 17:6, 19:1, and 21:25, you will read: "in those days, there was no king in Israel: every man did that which was right in his own eyes."

Now, look at the end of Ruth. Ruth 4:22 says, "Obed begat Jesse, and Jesse begat David." So, you see, this appendix of Judges gives us a good cross-section picture of the land in the days of the judges. It is very interesting to note, that the first story is in the North, the second story is in the central southside, and the third story of Ruth is in the southern section. So, in the appendix, we get, as it were, the cross-section of the whole land and we find that the key is: "there was no king, and every man did that which was right in his own eyes."

When there is no real authority, everyone does what they think is right. God's thought is always authority and authority always leads to stability and security. Now, of course, we are not talking about man's authority, we are talking primarily about the authority of God. The authority of God's Christ, once owned and recognised, rules out factions and brings in stability and security. This really is the key to this book. We find that in the last part of the appendix, it was all to do with this. Then the book of Ruth is there to show us how the king is provided in the sovereignty and grace of God.

Now go back from chapter 3 to chapter 16 and what do we find? As soon as the Lord has got authority in a man, there is deliverance. As soon as that man is dead, the people go to pieces and everything falls apart. So, in the days of Othniel, you find a great coming together. Then, when Othniel dies, everything falls apart. Then you go to the next chapter about Ehud, and once again everyone is drawn together and then it fails. Then Shamgar. Then Deborah and Barak. Then there was Gideon who could rally 30,000 adult men of war. The whole land united because the Lord was with them. So, it continues one after another.

The Authority of God

What is the key to the book of Judges? It is simply this: when the authority of God is recognised and the people of God commit themselves to His authority, then there is stability and security. As soon as they fight authority, as soon as they rebel against authority, as soon as they defect or divide, everything stops and breaks up. The key to this book is the question of authority, by its presence or by its lack. This is what Judges teaches. It teaches us as much by its lack as it does by its presence. When the authority of God is in a situation, it is strength. When the authority of God is not there, everything goes to pieces. This is absolutely true. It does not matter where it is, or where you find it, it is absolutely true.

So, I think we have found here that the key to this book is government. The key to this book is authority. I think I have safeguarded it by saying we are not talking about flesh and blood's authority, but we are talking about the authority of God. Sooner or later, we have to take the step from the authority of God's Christ in heaven to the authority of Christ vested in human vessels on earth. This is a step that many people of God are very uneasy with, but it is there in the Word of God. We have to learn by the Word of God, what the Word of God teaches about these very things. I think there is a lot there which we have to learn.

Now I did write up something of an outline[2] of this book of Judges. You will see that it is really a very simple outline. It has an introduction of roughly three chapters. It has an appendix from chapters 17–21, and possibly the book of Ruth as well. Then it has

2   See outline in study guide following this chapter

the story of the deliverances from Judges 3 through Judges 16. Those 14 chapters are taken up with the deliverances of God.

The Introduction: Giving Ground to the Enemy

Israel's Failure

I want you to notice in the introduction that there are three things. First of all, it tells us what Israel did *not* drive out. I think I have mentioned this quite a lot, so there is no need to stress it anymore except to say that this introduction is, as it were, the summary of this history. The key to it is simply "look, they did not drive them out." What they did not drive out became their defeat, their downfall. This is always true of spiritual experience. Where we stop and settle down is the measure of our defeat. We can never stop and settle down in the Christian life. If we dare to stop and settle down to things as they are, that is our defeat. Sooner or later, if the devil takes 40 or 60 years to do it, he will undo it. Some Christians, unfortunately, will not find out until they are in the glory, that the enemy has got them in this matter. They stop, and where they stopped, was not only the measure of their defeat and the measure of their life, but it is the measure of their inheritance. We have to recognise that.

The Result of Israel's Failure

The second thing we have to recognise is the result. There was a result here. What was the result? The result was simply this: what they left in the land and did not drive out, became within the source of temptation. Most of you must have had this experience. It is, I think, comparatively easy to flee our youthful lusts when it is from without. It is a comparatively easy thing to turn away from the temptation that is from without. It is one of the most difficult things in the world when there is ground given to temptation *inside* of us, which always opens the door. This is ground inside, but it must be dealt with.

You note that there are two things here, the Baalim and the Ashtaroth. The word Ashtaroth is a very unusual plural of Asherah, Ashtaroth, Ashera or Ashtoreth. Baal was the male side, the male deity, and Asherah was the female deity. Connected with these were the most licentious and the most immoral forms of worship. Consequently, it is notable for the people of God to actually join themselves and start to call things like Mount Hermon, Baal Hermon, and Gideon to be called Jerubbaal and things like that all the time. They did not seem to realise just how this evil crept into them and began to be interwoven. It was the most difficult thing amongst them to divide the two things—to say: "that is Jehovah—that is Baal." These two were brought together. We have to mention this because that is why the Lord is so much against the worship of Baal and the worship of Asherah. It is just simply because of the terrible immorality that was associated with it. It was not *just* idolatry. So let us remember this about Baal and Ashera in all the history that we have in the Word of God. In your Authorised version, [KJV] you have the word "grove[3]". That is not the right word. For that word "grove," always remember the name Asherah, the female deity, and remember what I have told you about her.

So, you see that the result was that because those nations were not driven out, there was ground within. Whilst that may, at the

---

3   In the KJV, "grove" is used in place of the word "Asherah." See Judges 6.

beginning, have been strictly avoided and excluded, sooner or later that ground was opened, and from it the enemy worked to the breaking down of God's people.

The Lord's Reaction to Israel's Failure

Then again, I want you to notice that the Lord's reaction was simply to give the people over to this practice in order to cure them of it. This is always the Lord's reaction. When there is something that we want badly, generally if we will not let it go, He will give it to us because He is big enough to give us much rope. Generally, we hang ourselves with the rope, and then in a right way we come back to the Lord. So you see, the Lord's reaction is, "Very well, the only way to cure it is to let the whole thing come out and let them have a double dose of it." Here in the book of Judges you have got simply what the people wanted. They wanted to settle down, they did not want to fight, and the Lord allowed them to do it.

The Deliverances of God

Now, what about the deliverances of God? This is just the introduction for these deliverances, but what about the deliverances? I think we can pick out one or two and just speak for a while about those one or two. Some of these judges we can see are passed over literally in a few verses and others are given a good deal more space.

Deborah — The Role of Sisters

The first one that is given any real space is Deborah. Now, this is very interesting for all the sisters that the first judge should be a lady and should not only be a lady or a sister, but that this sister should occupy such a place and a position. Nevertheless, it is very interesting that in the account of those who through faith overcame, we do not find Deborah. Instead, we find Barak is mentioned. Barak in the story is very secondary. Deborah is first, but when it comes to the Lord mentioning things in Hebrews 11, He mentions Barak and seemingly forgets Deborah.

What is the key to this? You will find the key in the whole attitude of Deborah. Now, let me say just a few words, (I fear lest I be murdered by the sisters afterward). Deborah is far from being evidence that ladies can do anything and everything, but is the very testimony and illustration of the place that sisters have in the economy of God. Here is a woman, because there was no man, who could be taken up by God and given one of the greatest places in her day and generation that anyone, even a man, could be given. Yet, if you read the story carefully, she refuses to usurp authority once. When Barak said to her, "You lead them," she said, "I will not. You go." He said, "I will not go unless you come." She said, "I will come, but you go. You go first, I will come."

Read through the story, and you find that all the time Deborah is behind Barak. She goes to him, and she says, "Up Barak, for this day the Lord has given them into your hands" but she does not say, "Barak, come with me! The Lord has given them into my hand." She says, "Barak, the Lord has given them into your hand. You go up there and I will wait" (see Judges chapter 4).

You see there is something that the Scripture calls modest and shamefast[4] (understand this word, for it is in the Scriptures) about Deborah, which was absolutely beautiful and becoming. This woman could become the prophetess of Israel and be called their mother and yet there is nothing about it that is the least bit unbecoming. When I read the story, it seems to be perfectly in keeping. I do not get that awful feeling that evidently some of the brothers have that this is surely something that should not really be in the Bible at all, that presents us with a lot of problems. There is something absolutely becoming about the place of Deborah in this story. She was with Barak; she was behind Barak, and I believe that in Hebrews 11 she was included in the triumph of Barak. Barak could never have done what he did or gotten where he got if it had not been for Deborah. But Deborah refused to take anything to herself. All the time she passed it over to Barak. This is a question of authority. This is the key to the book of Judges. Deborah shows us the place of sisters in God's economy—a great place, a big place, an influential place, and an effective place. And yet it is a place that is not the least bit brazen or cheap or out of order. Let us take note then of that.

Gideon—Characteristics of Leadership

Then we come to Gideon. What do we find about Gideon? When we come to Gideon from chapter 6 to chapter 9 we find some rather wonderful things. I am going to mention this to you because quite a bit of the record is given over to this one judge. First, we are

---

4 "In like manner, that women adorn themselves in modest apparel, with shamefastness and sobriety; not with braided hair, and gold or pearls or costly raiment;" - I Timothy 2:9

given the character of leadership (Judges 6:11–24). What do we find about leadership? What is the character of leadership?

Conscientiousness

First of all, you will notice this: long before Gideon was called, he was obviously a conscientious person. He was not a person that sat around and waited. He was obviously a very, very hard-working, conscientious, efficient type of fellow. We find that even when the angel of the Lord came to him, He found him hard at work.

Humility

Then, the second thing you will notice about Gideon is not only that he was a man of real conscientiousness and hard work, but you will also find that he was a very humble fellow. Evidently, whatever his hands found to do, he did with all his might. I think the Lord always looks for people like that, who if they are given the smallest job to do, put all their strength and energy into it. This was the kind of man that Gideon was. It is one of the characteristics of real leadership that you can do a small thing as fully, as energetically, as zealously, and as devotedly as you would do a big thing. This is one of the things the Lord looks for in His children. He looks for humility, a preparedness to be nothing. Gideon was not the least bit swell-headed. He did not think that He was anything. He thought he was the least. His father's family was the least in Manasseh, and he himself was nothing. Why should the Lord choose him?

A Willingness to be Consumed

I want you also to notice that it was not only humility. I noticed that he offers a burnt offering. This is the essential character of leadership. If you are prepared to be consumed, if you are prepared to be offered on the altar and every single bit to be utterly consumed—then you are, in God's sight a leader, whether you are a brother or whether you are a sister. This is the thing that holds so many back—a terrible sense of self-preservation, of fear. No, this can never, never come into leadership. Leadership is illustrated by the burnt offering. Something wholly burned. Something wholly consumed. So, you see, you have got something there, you have got the character of leadership.

Utter and Complete Devotion

Then, I want you to notice something else about this from Judges 6:26–32. You will find his utterness, his complete devotion. He did a thing that could have cost him his life. He cut down the altar of Baal and destroyed it. This was his father's altar, and it was the altar of the camp and as it were, the place of worship. He destroyed the whole thing. This showed his complete and utter devotion. He could not do it by day, so he did it by night. But the point about Gideon is that he was utterly willing. He went on absolutely and wholeheartedly for the Lord.

Gideon's Fleece—A Picture of Leadership

The next thing I want you to notice about this is the confirmation of his call. What does this mean? Firstly, he says, "Lord, I will put a fleece out tonight. If the fleece is full of dew and the ground all around is dry, I will know You have spoken." The Lord did it.

Then he said, "Now, Lord, the next night I shall put out a fleece and I want You to make it absolutely bone-dry and all the ground around it dew." What does this speak about? (See Judges 6:36–40). It speaks again of the character of leadership.

First of all, when everything else around us is absolutely barren and bone-dry, the Lord would have us full of heavenly dew. Full of life, full of the water of life. Full of it. Absolutely full. This is leadership. When everyone else is like dying ducks, the leadership has got something to give. It is something inward, something that you cannot put your finger on, but it is there. You have got it. But the other side is a paradox. Leadership—it always has a great sense of being bone-dry when everything around it has got the benefit. First, you fill the fleece with dew, then you get the dew out of it and everything else benefits. This is the paradox. Death in us–life in you. "Always bearing about in the body the dying of Jesus that life also may be manifested" (see II Corinthians 4:10). What is the next thing? Death worketh in us, life in you. So, this is the character of leadership according to God. That we should draw and learn how to draw on God so that we have got life inside when everything else is barren. Then to know what it is to walk by faith so that when we feel bone-dry, everyone else can know the benefit of our walk with God. This must always be the character of divine leadership.

Corporate Pioneering—Watchfulness

Then I want you all to notice in chapter 7 the character of corporate pioneering. Personal leadership to corporate pioneering, or corporate leadership. What do we find in Joshua 7:4–8?

We find that they are eliminated from 32,000 to 300. How does he do it? First of all, he says, "Now look here all of you," the Lord says to him, "Tell them all, 'all those of you who want to go, you can go,'" (I have often wondered what would happen if we did that.) "Very well, those of you who do not want to go on, you may leave. If you want your homes, your careers, your happiness, your own life, you go. Leave us to it." And a very large number went.

Then the Lord said to him, "There are far too many. Take them down to the river. When they come to the river, watch how they drink. Those that get down and lap up the water with their tongue are not to be taken. Those that scoop it up and drink it, take them." What was this about? What is this character in corporate pioneering the Lord is looking for? A corporate watchfulness. It would have been the easiest thing, to say, "Well, look here at all these others, they will watch. I can stoop and drink while they watch" As some of us pointed out, it was rather selfish of those who had their fill and put their faces almost into it. They were first to the water, and they drank their fill. But it is very easy in a company to think, "Well, so-and-so will watch, I do not have to, they are bound to. In all this crowd here, goodness gracious, if an enemy comes, someone will tell us in no time." That is the kind of thing the Lord says cannot be in corporate pioneering. Every single one has got to have such a watchful care over one another that not one of them would dare do it even if there were 30,000. They would all be, as we say, on the *qui vive*. All on the watch. All waiting. All alert. This is a characteristic of corporate pioneering.

Corporate Pioneering— Essentials for Victory

Then what were the other essential things for victory? If in corporate pioneering we are to know victory, there are three essential things. First, there must be a trumpet, secondly, there must be a pitcher, and thirdly, there must be a torch that is alight. But I have left out the most important detail. The pitcher must be broken. Gideon told them that they were all to take a trumpet and a pitcher and put a torch inside the pitcher. Then, at the given signal, they were to blow the trumpet, smash the pitcher, pick up the torch, and shout. What does this speak of? It speaks of this: in corporate pioneering, there is an absolute obedience to the Word of God—to the voice of God. There must be a preparedness to be utterly shattered in living together. I might point out that the shattering is done by one another. There are very few people who shatter themselves. It is brother so-and-so and sister so-and-so that shatters us. That is the way it happens that the light inside can be seen. This is always the way to victory in corporate pioneering. If we are pioneering the way, this is the way. We must be absolutely alert to the voice of God and prepared to sound it out without fear. We must be prepared to be shattered so that the light inside may get out to others. This then is really, simply the message of Judges.

4.
Judges
Study Guide

Introduction

Judges belongs to the second section of the Bible, called in the Hebrew canon *The Prophets* and in ours *The Historical Books*.

Judges is almost a complete contrast to Joshua. In Joshua, we see the people of God inheriting, but in Judges we see a continual cycle of declension, division, defection, disorder, confusion, and then repentance and deliverance. There seems to be no progress of real worth, unless we look upon the book of Ruth as part of Judges. It is a wearying cycle, even though in all the failure of God's people, we find the mercy and faithfulness of God. In God's revelation of His purpose, however, the book of Judges is another step forward. We begin to see the need for authority emphasised. Apart from the Tabernacle at Shiloh, there was no central authority, spiritual or civil. In Israel—"every man did that which was right in his own eyes." Any loyalty that did exist was tribal, rather than to the entire nation. In this state of disorder, there was not only disunity and fragmentation, but the people of God became vulnerable to the inroads of pagan religion and intermarriage.

Authorship and Date

No one knows the author, and there are many conflicting views, but Jewish tradition ascribes it to Samuel. According to Jewish tradition, Samuel wrote Judges, Ruth and part of I Samuel. The style throughout the book suggests that one person was the author, although it would also appear that he used older records.

It seems apparent from the phrase "in those days there was no king in Israel," that it was not written before the first monarchy (Saul). See Judges 17:6; 18:1; 19:1; 21:25. From Judges 1:21 and II Samuel 5:6–10, it seems obvious that it was written before Jerusalem became capital (1000 BC.) These facts could well argue for Samuel's authorship of this book.

We can therefore say that Judges was written some time between 1400 BC and 1000 BC. It covers the period between the death of Joshua, after the conquest of the land, to the times of Eli just prior to the introduction of the monarchy in Israel, a total of about 300 years.

It ought to be remembered that these "Judges" are not necessarily consecutive. Some may have been contemporary. The two stories in chapters 17–21, and Ruth can be dated with the earlier part of Judges.

Especial Note

The Rabbinic chronology for this period was formed on the basis that one generation equaled forty years.
Hence:

1 generation in the wilderness		=	*40 years*
8 generations of the Judges		=	*320 years*
1 generation of Eli		=	*40 years*
1 generation of Samuel		=	*40 years*
1 generation of David		=	*40 years*
	Total	=	*480 years*

Key to the Book

We ought to note that the writer gives us three reasons in Judges 2:20–3:6, for this phase of Israel's history.

1. To visit their disobedience	*Judges 2:20–23*
2. To prove Israel	*Judges 2:22; 3:4*
3. To teach them to war	*Judges 3:2*

Thus we see the record of failure and deliverance throughout this book. It is the story of failures leading to deliverances only because of the mercy and faithfulness of God. We see also, the Lord taking the defeat, the failure and the misery of His people, and using it all to instruct them and us, and to work out His own purpose. Indeed, finally to provide a king.

We need also to recognise that Judges is a book of "causes and effects." All defeat and declension etc., as well as all revival and renewal is traced to some simple beginning. In principle it is always to do with either the rejection of God's authority or the recognition of it. See Nehemiah's prayer, Nehemiah 9:24–27, which is an enlightening commentary on this.

The key to this book is contained in these verses: Judges 17:6; 18:1, 7; 19:1; 21:25. It is the absolute necessity of divine authority. All is traced to this, to either its presence or its absence. The Hebrew word translated "judges" from which we get the title for this book, simply means "judge," "lawgiver," or "governor." These Judges represent divine authority and government. It is therefore instructive to note that this authority leads to deliverance. They are called *saviours* or *deliverers* (see Judges 2:16, 18; 3:9, 10, 15 and compare to Nehemiah 9:27). How interesting it is to note that the New Testament opens with the presentation of Christ our Saviour as King.

It is instructive to note that if Ruth is part of Judges, it leads to the provision of a king (see Ruth 4:22). We ought also to note that there are 12 Judges, a highly significant number in Scripture, representing government or authority.

Outline of the Book

The book of Ruth has often been closely connected with Judges, and certainly there are some interesting points to consider. Whatever the truth of the matter is, Ruth has been placed after Judges in our Bible.

The outline of Judges is very simple:

    I. An Introduction: Judges 1:1–3:6

    II. The Deliverances of the Lord: Judges 3:7–16

III. An Appendix: Judges 17–21, and perhaps Ruth

An Introduction: Judges 1:1–3:6

Partial Possession—the cause of defeat and failure

A. What Israel did not drive out: Judges 1:1–2:10

B. The result: Judges 2:11–15

C. The Lord's reaction: Judges 2:16–3:6

The Deliverances of the Lord: Judges 3:7–16

We ought to note:

A. Note that all these deliverances begin with God finding a person who will do His will (see Judges 2:16, 18; 3:9–10). The measure in which that man or woman is given to, and obedient to the Lord, governs the depth and duration of the deliverance.

B. Note that we have the record of seven periods of apostasy and declension, and the Lord's deliverances, in answer to the cry of His own people.

i. First Apostasy: Judges 3:7–11

Locality:	South Israel
Punishment:	Eight years' subjection to Mesopotamia

First deliverance:

Deliverer:	Othniel of Judah
Peace:	40 years

ii. Second Apostasy: Judges 3:12–31

Locality:	Central Israel
Punishment:	18 years subjection to Moab (helped by Ammon and Amalek)

Second Deliverance:

Deliverer:	Ehud of Benjamin and after him Shamgar
Peace:	80 years

iii. Third Apostasy: Judges 4:1–5:31

Locality: North Israel

Punishment: 20 years' subjection to the Canaanites.

Third Deliverance:

Deliverers: Deborah of Ephraim, Barak of Naphtali

Peace: 40 years

iv. Fourth Apostasy: Judges 6:1–8:32

Locality: Central Israel

Punishment: 7 years subjection to Midian
              (helped by Amalek and the children of the East)

Fourth Deliverance:

Deliverer: Gideon of Manasseh

Peace: 40 Years

v. Fifth Apostasy: Judges 8:33–10:5

Localities: Central Israel and East of Jordan

Punishment: 3 years under Abimelech (son of Gideon)

Fifth Deliverance:

Deliverers: Tola of Issachar, Jair of Gad

Peace: 45 years

vi. Sixth Apostasy: Judges 10:6–12:15

Locality: East of Jordan, North and Central Israel

Punishment: 18 years' subjection to Philistia and Ammon

Sixth Deliverance:

Deliverers: Jephthah of Gad
              Ibzam of Judah
              Elon of Zebulun
              Abdon of Ephraim

Peace: 31 years

vii. Seventh Apostasy: Judges 13:1–16:31

    Locality: ?

    Punishment: 40 years' subjection to the Philistines.

    Seventh Deliverance

    Deliverer: Samson of Dan

    Peace: 20 years

    Note: on Gideon (from fourth deliverance)

- Note the character of his leadership.

    a) The call of Gideon: Judges 6:11–24 (Conscientiousness, humility, the burnt offering–all consumed)

    b) Utterness of his devotion: Judges 6:25–32

    c) The confirmation: Judges 6:36–40 (its meaning–the Cross)

- Note the character of corporate pioneering.

    a) The large number cut down to three hundred: Judges 7:4–8 (Mark the way many were eliminated)

    b) The essential way of victory: Judges 7:15–23 (Trumpet, Pitchers, Torches–the essentials in overcoming)

    c) Wrong attitudes: Judges 8:1–21

        Men of Ephraim

        Men of Succoth

- The end of Gideon: Judges 8:22–32

    a) His humility

    b) The Ephod and the result

    c) Abimelech

Note on Jephthah of Gad (from sixth deliverance)

- He understood history: Judges 11:12–28
- He made a foolish vow: Judges 11:29–31

- He was devoted to the Lord, but not fully according to truth. There was a mixture in him: Judges 11:22–40

Note on Samson of Dan (from seventh deliverance):
- A Nazirite–the first recorded one.
- The burnt offering: Judges 13:15–20
- The weakness and strength of Samson
- His end

III. An Appendix–confusion and the grace of God. Judges 17–21 and Ruth

Three stories that reveal the condition of the land, (one from the North, one from Central Israel, one from the South.) The first two reveal a sad state of confusion, evil and depravity as a consequence of falling away from the Lord. The last reveals the grace of God, shining through all the misery and disorder.

A. A picture of unfaithfulness to the Lord: Judges 17–18

B. A picture of depravity among the people: Judges 19–21

C. A picture of purity and faithfulness;
God sovereignly fulfilling his purpose–Ruth

In all this we notice one thing which is clearly brought out in these last three stories—authority is the key to stability, unity and progress.

Message of the Book

The land or, to use the New Testament phrase, "The Heavenlies," is the sphere of the spiritual experience of God's people in Christ. Possessing the land is to enter in to what is ours in Christ, to make what is potential, actual in our experience. It is a stern and long-drawn out battle with the enemy, (cf. Ephesians 6:10-18). The book of Judges reveals some of the perils which can beset the people of God as they seek to possess their possessions. E.g. compromise, disunity, defection, isolation, disorder, allowing enemy strongholds to remain, etc. etc. The fact is that whatever is undealt with in our personal lives, or corporate life, becomes our undoing. The enemy sees to that. All these matters are only dealt with when the King comes into His place of authority. The only answer is His absolute Lordship and our total obedience.

The authority of God's Christ is absolutely essential to stability and security. Where the kingship of God's Christ is not recognised, or recognised only in name, the result is always disorder and confusion, whether personal or corporate. We need, afresh, therefore, to recognise the kingship of Christ. Then we need to see how that authority is vested in men. In the midst of all the failure and the tragedy of unsettled issues, God's way is to deliver and to answer by a fresh recognition of His authority on our part, and a fresh committal to it. Then, and then alone, do we know peace and rest; we enter into the fullness and reality of our so great salvation.

Recommended Books

The Foundations of Bible History: Joshua, Judges - John Garstang
Judges and Ruth - A. Cundall & L. Morris
Israel in Canaan under Joshua & the Judges - A. Edersheim

Questions

1. State the purpose for which God raised up different judges, and state why it was necessary that these judges be raised up.

2. Sum up in one or two sentences the contrast between the message of the book of Joshua and that of Judges.

3. What are the reasons for God's raising up of nations to try Israel? (See Judges 2:16–3:7)

4. What are the main lessons you have learned from the life of Samson? Can you find any likenesses to Christ from his life?

5. Write, in your own words, about half a page on what you have learned about the need for authority from the book of Judges.

6. What do you learn about the state of the morals and religion in Israel from the appendix of the book of Judges? Which verses in these chapters were given as a commentary upon the situation?

7. How many of the names in Judges can you find in Hebrews 11? Why were they included in that chapter?

8. In what way does the book of Judges show us God working out His purpose?

9. What do you learn about leadership and corporate pioneering from this book of Judges?

10. State in one or two sentences the supreme facts about God which you have learned from the book of Judges.

5.
Ruth Study Guide

Introduction

In a background of defeat and division, of carnage, depravity and brutality, we find the story of Ruth as one of the most beautiful in the Bible. It would seem from this story that war and strife were far away rather than the every-day experience of the people. None the less, the books of Ruth and Judges belong to the same time. Indeed, it is instructive to see the way in which Ruth is linked with Judges. In Joshua, we have seen the people inheriting the land and settling down. In Judges, we have seen the vital need for authority if there is to be unity and stability. Ruth shows us the way in which the Lord, in the midst of defeat and failure, is sovereignly working to provide a king. In this sense, the book of Ruth is the link between the book of Judges, on the one hand, and the books of Samuel and Kings, on the other hand.

Historically, the main and consecutive (although not wholly consecutive) part of the narrative in Judges and Ruth is found in

Judges 3–16. Judges 17–21 and the book of Ruth describe three undated episodes which took place during the time covered by Judges 3–16. One in Dan in the North concerning Micah, (Judges 17–18), and one in Shiloh, in central Israel, concerning an unnamed Levite (Judges 19–21), and one in Bethlehem, in the South concerning Ruth. Ruth is undoubtedly the most important.

Out of the seemingly endless cycle of defeat in the book of Judges, we find, in Ruth, that the Lord is moving forward once again. This time He moves forward to the establishing of divine authority among His people in the provision of a king after His own heart.

Ruth is one of the two books of the Bible that bear the name of women. The other book is Esther. These two women are remarkable for the way in which they contrast with one another. Ruth also is one of the five women mentioned in the genealogy of the Lord Jesus, (Matthew 1:2–16). Two of these women were of one-time doubtful morals—Rahab and Bathsheba. Four of them, it would seem, were Gentiles or foreigners—Tamar, Rahab, Ruth, and Bathsheba. So often God surprises us in His choice of the men and women through whom He accomplishes His purpose.

Authorship and Date

There is no indication as to who is the author of the book of Ruth, but the Talmud tells us, "Samuel wrote his own book and Judges and Ruth." This might well be true, for Samuel was the last of the Judges and was the instrument used by God for bringing in the monarchy. Since he anointed David as the man after God's own heart, he may well have been led of the Spirit of God to trace David's family history.

Certainly the book of Ruth must have been written in its present form after David's accession to the throne, (compare Ruth 1:1 with 4:17, 22. Mark this, "When the judges ruled.") So it would have been written shortly after 1000 BC. It is quite possible that an older document underlies the book that we now have.

The book of Ruth does not chronologically follow the book of Judges. In fact, the events described in Ruth took place at the beginning of the Judges period. The famine in the land, Ruth 1:1, may refer to the famine in Gideon's day (see Judges 6:1–6).

Key to the Book

If we see Ruth as being linked with Judges, particularly the last chapters 17–21, we shall remember the oft repeated phrase in that book: "there was no king in Israel." Everything in Judges is traced to the absolute necessity for divine authority, either to its presence or its absence. Ruth is the story of the way in which the Lord, in the midst of all the failure and disgrace of His people, sovereignly works to provide a king. In fact it is the story of how He uses that failure and breakdown to work out His own purpose. Ruth ends with another major step forward in the purpose of God—a king. The book begins with a famine and ends with David (Ruth 1:1 cp. 4:22).

However, we need to look even more deeply. Ruth teaches us the simple lesson that God must have His means, if He is to provide the king. It is this that brings us to the key—steadfast faith. The sovereignty of God is linked, in His wondrous wisdom and grace, with the faith of His children—a divinely given faith, which works by a divinely begotten love. A king is going to be provided, but this will come about, not only by the sovereign working of God, but also by the steadfast faithful cooperation of His own. This is no cheap or easy way, but a costly matter to those involved.

Especial Note

Whilst we believe the main teaching of Ruth is as above, many rightly see this book as a beautiful picture of the sinner and the Saviour. Boaz as the kinsman redeemer is the type of Christ. Ruth, the Moabitess shut out by the law, is the type of the sinner. She is influenced by the testimony of a saint (Naomi) and is drawn back with her to the land. There she meets her kinsman redeemer who can meet all her needs and makes her claim on him in simple dependence (3:9). His response is immediate (3:11). Their union and fruitfulness results in the coming of the king and the kingdom.

Outline of the Book

I. The breakdown of faith and its consequences: Ruth 1:1–5
  A. Famine conditions in the promised land: Ruth 1:1–2
    i. Was this to test them? Gideon did not depart from the land because of it. See Judges 6 cp. Genesis 12:10–20.
    ii. Unbelief always follows natural reasoning. It would not have been wrong to go down to Moab if the Lord had directed them, but did He?

iii. It is interesting to note that these believers left their inheritance in the land, left Bethlehem (House of Bread) for Moab.

iv. Note the meaning of Elimelech: "My God is King." It appears that he contradicted his name.

B. Ten years of loss: Ruth 1:3–5

i. What was the outcome of their departure, of following natural reasoning?

ii. The death of Elimelech; the marriage of his sons to unbelievers; the death of both his sons.

iii. Unbelief always leads to compromises and death; faith always leads to fruitfulness and life.

iv. It was an ancient Hebrew belief that if there was no seed to keep the father's name alive, it was a terrible shame and reproach, and evidence of divine displeasure. See Ruth 1:5 and compare to Ruth 1:13, 21. thus Naomi's deep suffering. See Ruth 1:19, 20 (Naomi—pleasantness; Mara—bitterness.)

II.   Faith, Tried and Refined: Ruth 1:6–22

A. The best commentary on these verses is found in I Peter 1:6–9; Romans 10:17; (cp Ruth 1:6) II Corinthians 5:7; Galatians 5:6

B. Ruth and Orpah decide to return: Ruth 1:6–7

C. Naomi's plea and their reaction: Ruth 1:8–10

D. Naomi's second plea: Ruth 1:11–13

E. Orpah's response: Ruth 1:14—Faith mixed with self-interest, she kisses Naomi and departs!

F. Ruth's response: Ruth 1:14—steadfast faith—she clung to Naomi!

G. Naomi's third plea: Ruth 1:15

H. Ruth's confession: Ruth 1:16–17—Faith alone. No prospect but loneliness, ostracism (Deuteronomy 23:3) and poverty.

I. They return to Bethlehem at the Passover: Ruth 1:18–22

III. Faith overcoming: Ruth 2:3

A. The best commentary on these verses is found in 1 Timothy 6:12; 1 John 5:4–5

B. Ruth's work—hard, routine, ordinary.

C. She sought it herself cf.—Ruth 2:2, 7, 17.

D. Her main concern was Naomi—selflessness— Ruth 2:11, 18.

E. Her simplicity of obedience and her humility. Note that she acted in fellowship. Ruth 2:2, 10, 13; 3:5.

F. The sovereignty of God in guidance, 2:3—and in provision See Ruth 2:8–9, 14.

G. The near kinsman—Boaz and the claiming of her right: Ruth 3:6–13 cp. Deuteronomy 25:5–10; Mark 12:19–22. Here we have a most beautiful picture of Christ as our kinsman redeemer. Kinsman, for He became man. Redeemer because He is the only One with the right and power to redeem.

IV. Faith inheriting: Ruth 4

A. The best commentary on these verses is found in Hebrews 6:12

B. The redemption: Ruth 4:1–12

C. The marriage and the child. Ruth 4:13–16

D. The end—a king: Ruth 4:17–22

E. Divinely given faith has drawn Ruth right into the sovereign purpose of God to provide the King, great David's greater Son. Note from Jacob to David is 12 generations. Boaz and Ruth are the ninth. Ruth, the Moabitess, has come into the Messianic line. See Luke 3:23–34, especially verse 32 cp. Matthew 1:5.

F. It is also very moving to note that it is through Boaz, the lord of the harvest (2:3) the kinsman redeemer (2:20), that Ruth, the Moabitess shut out by the law, having no part with the people of God, or in the purpose of God, finds redemption and a place in the Kingdom.

Message of the Book

The message of Ruth is simply that in days of decline and breakdown God is at work sovereignly to answer the situation and fulfil His purpose. He does not merely work in a detached way but takes the very failure and breakdown and uses them to bring deliverance and victory. The one thing He looks for in the instrument He uses is faith. Steadfast faith gives God His way and prepares the way for the coming King. Such faith unites us with the throne.

Recommended Books

The Marraige of Ruth - H. H. Rowqley
Judges and Ruth - A. Cundall & L. Morris
The Plot of the Book of Ruth - E. Robertson

Study Guide Questions

1. When was the book of Ruth written, and when did Ruth live?

2. What is the key to this book? Give verses to illustrate your answer.

3. What is the main thing which God is doing in this book, and how does this fit in with the book of Judges and with 1 Samuel?

4. Write a paragraph describing the changing fortunes of Naomi in the book of Ruth. Does this teach you anything about the way in which God sometimes deals with His children?

5. Do you learn any spiritual lesson from the way in which Boaz receives Ruth in chapter 3?

6. What would you say is the main lesson in Ruth 1:6–18?

7. What Old Testament laws were being applied in Ruth 2:2, 7; 3:6–9; 4:1–12? Give Scripture references.

8. What do you learn about "inheritance" from the book of Ruth?

9. Ruth was a Moabitess. Does this say anything to you about God's eternal purpose? (See Ephesians 2:11–22, Ephesians 3:1–11).

10. What do you most admire about the woman Ruth?

11. What are the consequences of an evil heart of unbelief, (natural reasoning, and "leaning upon our own understanding") as we see it in Elimelech and Naomi?

12. Abraham went to Egypt because of famine and found trouble (Genesis 12:10–20); Jacob went to Egypt because of famine and was greatly blessed. (Genesis 46:1–49:33) What is the difference? Should we ever let famine dictate our movements?

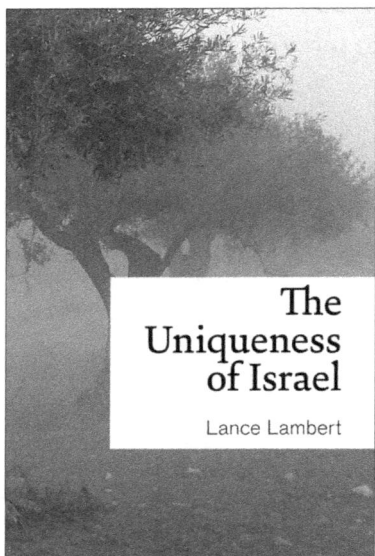

The Uniqueness of Israel

Woven into the fabric of Jewish existence there is an undeniable uniqueness. There is bitter controversy over the subject of Israel, but time itself will establish the truth about this nation's place in God's plan. For Lance Lambert, the Lord Jesus is the key that unlocks Jewish history He is the key not only to their fall, but also to their restoration. For in spite of the fact that they rejected Him, He has not rejected them.

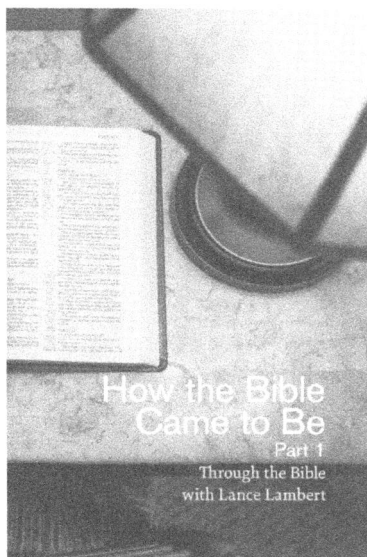

How the Bible Came to Be: Part 1

How is the Bible still as applicable in the 21st century as it was when it was first penned? How did so many authors, with different backgrounds and over thousands of years, write something so perfectly fitting with one another?

Lance Lambert breaks down these, and many other questions in this first volume of his series teaching through the Bible. He lays a firm foundation for going on to study the Word of the living God.

And ye shall seek me, and find me, when ye shall search for me with all your heart.
Jeremiah 29:13

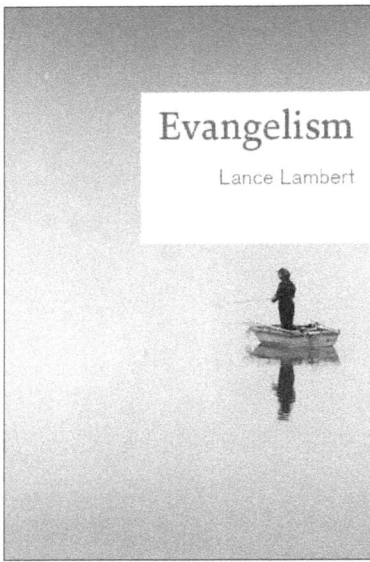

Evangelism

What is God's purpose in evangelism?

It is clear that the Word of God commands us to preach the gospel to every creature, to go into the whole world and make disciples of all nations baptising them in the name of the Father, the Son and the Holy Spirit.

So how do we do it?

In "Evangelism" Lance opens the scriptures to reveal how the church can practically and effectively preach the gospel to the unsaved world, by revealing to them in scripture their need for a Saviour, the work of the Saviour, and how to receive the Saviour. He explains practical means of winning souls and how to follow-up with the newly saved to make disciples of the Lord Jesus. Evangelism is the way by which we gather the materials for the house of God.

So faith comes by hearing, and hearing through the word of Christ.

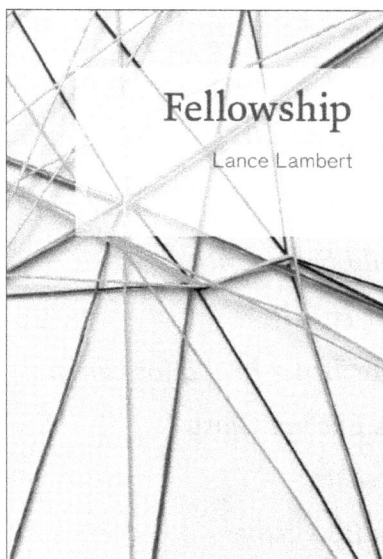

Fellowship
Lance Lambert

Fellowship

Ephesians 2 says that we in the household of God are to be built up together for a habitation for God in the Spirit.

What does this mean for you and me to be built up together with other believers? How should we contribute to the building work of Christ? What are the principles that govern this fellowship and building work?

In this current volume, Lance Lambert addresses these and other questions. He shares how "God has always desired a dwelling place in which He can express Himself, reveal Himself and manifest Himself, as it were, a place in which He can find His home."

Thank the Lord this is His heart's desire—to be with us and let us know Him. How blessed we are!

Find more books by Lance Lambert on lancelambert.org

Qualities of God's Servants

Reigning with Christ

Spiritual Character

Talks with Leaders

The Battle of the Ages

The Eternal Purpose of God

The Glory of God: Reflections from Exodus 33

The Glory of Thy People Israel

The Gospel of the Kingdom

The Importance of Covering

The Last Days and God's Priorities

The Prize

The Relevance of Biblical Prophecy

The Silent Years

The Supremacy of Jesus

The Uniqueness of Israel

The Way to the Eternal Purpose of God

They Shall Mount up with Wings

Thine Is the Power

Thou Art Mine

Through the Bible with Lance Lambert: Genesis - Deuteronomy

Till the Day Dawns

Unity : Behold How Good and How Pleasant - Ministries from Psalm 133

Warring the Good Warfare

What Is God Doing?: Lessons from Church History

www.ingramcontent.com/pod-product-compliance
Lightning Source LLC
Chambersburg PA
CBHW061151040426

42445CB00013B/1646